Nat & Alex Wolff

ABDO
Publishing Company

A Big Buddy Book
by **Sarah Tieck**

VISIT US AT
www.abdopublishing.com

Published by ABDO Publishing Company, 8000 West 78th Street, Edina, Minnesota 55439.

Copyright © 2009 by Abdo Consulting Group, Inc. International copyrights reserved in all countries. No part of this book may be reproduced in any form without written permission from the publisher. Buddy Books™ is a trademark and logo of ABDO Publishing Company.

Printed in the United States.

Coordinating Series Editor: Rochelle Baltzer
Contributing Editors: Heidi M.D. Elston, Megan M. Gunderson, Marcia Zappa
Graphic Design: Maria Hosley
Cover Photograph: AP Photo: Jennifer Graylock
Interior Photographs/Illustrations: AP Photo: AP Photo (page 11), Jim Cooper (pages 5, 29), Eyewire/Cities of America CD (page 9), Shiho Fukada (page 13), Jennifer Graylock (page 7), Peter Kramer (page 19), NBC NewsWire via AP Images/Virginia Sherwood (page 21), Mark J. Terrill (page 17); Getty Images: WireImage/Larry Busacca (page 24), WireImage/Jesse Grant (page 23), Getty Images for Nickelodeon/Scott Gries (page 14), WireImage/Janette Pellegrini (page 25), Thos Robinson (page 17), Time Life Pictures/Ted Thai (page 11), Getty Images for Nickelodeon/Kevin Winter (page 14); Photos.com (pages 9, 27, 29).

Library of Congress Cataloging-in-Publication Data

Tieck, Sarah, 1976-
  Nat & Alex Wolff / Sarah Tieck.
     p. cm. -- (Big buddy biographies)
  Includes index.
  ISBN 978-1-60453-126-8
  1. Wolff, Nat, 1994- 2. Wolff, Alex, 1997- 3. Naked Brothers Band. 4. Rock musicians--United States--Biography.
I. Title.

ML3930.W63T54 2008
782.42164092'2--dc22
[B]
                              2008010634

Contents

Rising Stars

Nat and Alex Wolff are musicians and actors. They are best known as the stars of *The Naked Brothers Band*.

The Naked Brothers Band is a popular television show. It first appeared in February 2007 on Nickelodeon. Since then, millions of people around the world have watched it.

On *The Naked Brothers Band,* Nat *(left)* is the band's lead singer and keyboard player. Alex *(right)* sings and plays the drums.

Family Ties

Nat and Alex are brothers. Nathaniel Marvin "Nat" Wolff was born on December 17, 1994. Alexander Draper "Alex" Wolff was born on November 1, 1997. Their parents are Polly Draper and Michael Wolff.

THE BROTHER'S BAND

Did you know...

Alex's middle name is his mother's last name.

The Wolffs often attend events together. Sometimes their cousin Jesse Draper *(far right)* joins them. She plays Jesse Cook on *The Naked Brothers Band.*

7

Where in the World?

CANADA

N
W E
S

NEW YORK

PACIFIC
OCEAN

CALIFORNIA

UNITED STATES

New York City

Los Angeles

ATLANTIC
OCEAN

MEXICO

Nat was born in Los Angeles, California.
Alex was born in New York City, New York.
The family lives in an apartment in Manhattan.
Manhattan is part of New York City.

New York City *(above)* and Los Angeles *(below)* are big cities. Both cities are known for supporting the arts, including acting and singing.

Famous Parents

Nat and Alex are not the only stars in their family. Their parents were also on television!

Polly is an actress and a movie writer. In the late 1980s, she acted in a popular show called *thirtysomething.*

Michael is a famous jazz musician. He was on *The Arsenio Hall Show* from 1989 to 1994. Michael led the television show's band.

Michael (*above left*) met Polly when she appeared on *The Arsenio Hall Show* in 1989. They soon fell in love and got married.

Polly (*above left*) has been in magazines and on television. She is famous for her work on *thirtysomething*.

Did you know...

After the September 11 attacks, Nat wanted to help the New York City firefighters. So, he and his mom put together a benefit concert. The concert earned more than $46,000!

Before They Were Stars

Despite having famous parents, Nat and Alex had a normal childhood. They spent time with friends and played with their dog, E.T.

Fame hasn't changed the Wolffs much. Nat says the main difference is that people recognize them. He likes knowing people listen to his music.

The Wolff brothers mostly taught themselves to play instruments. Nat *(left)* took some piano lessons. But, Alex *(right)* learned the drums on his own. He just watched Beatles drummer Ringo Starr play on television!

Nat and Alex both love listening to music
and playing instruments. In preschool, Nat
started his own band with friends. Alex loves
the rock-and-roll band the Beatles. This led
him to play the drums.

Starting Out

Nat wanted to be an actor for many years. He even hung signs on his door to let his parents know. The signs said, "I want to be a child actor." At first, Nat's parents said no. They both worked in show business and knew it was hard. Michael and Polly wanted their kids to have normal lives.

Today, the entire Wolff family works on *The Naked Brothers Band*. In addition, Michael is still a well-known jazz musician. And, Polly continues to act.

Finally, Nat's mom said he could make a pretend documentary. Together, they created *The Naked Brothers Band: The Movie* in 2005.

It follows the lives of a fake, world-famous rock band. Nat and Alex were the stars. Polly asked some of her famous friends to be in it, too.

Uma Thurman acted in the pretend documentary. Some of Polly's friends from *thirtysomething* also appeared.

Television Stars

Nickelodeon wanted to make *The Naked Brothers Band: The Movie* into a television series. So, the Wolffs started working on a show. The show follows the band members as they practice, perform, and handle everyday problems.

Nat and Alex star in it and write all the songs. Michael plays their dad on the show. Polly writes, directs, and produces the show.

In 2008, the Naked Brothers Band appeared on the *Today* show. They performed their well-known song "I Don't Want to Go to School."

The cast of *The Naked Brothers Band* are good friends. The group plays video games and basketball together. They have fun on the **set**, too. Some cast members were even part of Nat's childhood band!

David Levi, Qaasim Middleton, Thomas Batuello, Allie DiMeco, and Cooper Pilot are part of *The Naked Brothers Band* cast.

Off the Set

Nat and Alex have appeared in magazines and on television.

The Naked Brothers Band is a success. Some of Nat and Alex's songs have become very popular. And, there are many Naked Brothers Band products. These include books, shirts, and CDs.

Nat and Alex are becoming famous. But, they still attend school and do homework. Nat and Alex even have bedtimes! But, they are allowed to stay up late to write songs.

Buzz

Nat and Alex's first album was **released** in 2007. It is called *The Naked Brothers Band*. In April 2008, they released *I Don't Want to Go to School*.

The show began its second successful season in 2008. The new season follows the band's tour. Fans are excited to see what is next for Nat and Alex Wolff.

The cast of *The Naked Brothers Band* travels to make the show. Nat was excited to see places such as New Orleans, Louisiana *(right)*. His dad had played jazz there.

Snapshot

⭐ **Names**: Nathaniel Marvin Wolff, Alexander Draper Wolff

⭐ **Birthdays**: December 17, 1994 (Nat), November 1, 1997 (Alex)

⭐ **Birthplaces**: Los Angeles, California (Nat), New York City, New York (Alex)

⭐ **Home**: New York City, New York

⭐ **Starred in**: *The Naked Brothers Band: The Movie, The Naked Brothers Band*

⭐ **Albums**: *The Naked Brothers Band, I Don't Want to Go to School*

Important Words

documentary a movie or a television program that presents facts, often about an event or a person.

produce to oversee the making of a movie, a play, an album, or a radio or television show.

release to make available to the public.

set the place where a movie or a television show is recorded.

Web Sites

To learn more about Nat and Alex Wolff, visit ABDO Publishing Company on the World Wide Web. Web sites about Nat and Alex Wolff are featured on our Book Links page. These links are routinely monitored and updated to provide the most current information available.

www.abdopublishing.com

Index